THE BODY IS
THE PATH

Ashley Lauren

ABOUT THE AUTHOR

Ashley Lauren is a poet, mother, and truth-teller living on a farm in rural North Dakota. Her writing explores the intersections of trauma, healing, and love through deeply embodied, heart-led verse. The Body is the Path is her debut collection.

CONTENTS

Part I: The Body is the Path

Part II: Let Yourself be Swallowed Whole

Part III: Sacred Work

Part IV: Wild and Unbound

PART I: THE BODY IS THE PATH

"The wound is the place where the Light enters you."
Rumi

THE BODY IS THE PATH

I discovered a few years ago
that I could not trust my own thinking.

Sort of a horrifying thought
given our highly intellectualized
state of the world.

My thinking was polluted
with my nervous system responses
after years of fighting
through dysfunctional relationships,
friendships, and work dynamics
and a brain wired since childhood
for protection not connection
left me in a space where
I had no idea what was
healthy or not,
fear or intuition,
reality or not.

My old way of being was entirely faulty at best.

It was simply impossible
to tell if my impulsive action
was driven from true gut knowing
or because I was repeating
an old trauma loop,
familiar and conditioned.

I began operating under the premise
that all my thoughts were false.
Every last one of them needed reevaluation.

It was deliverance from the old me.

My life became like a choose-your-own adventure
book.

I began to meet each person,
situation,
or moment,
with total curiosity.

What do I feel?
What is coming up?
Is this thought bullshit?
What about the next one?

If I used to do this
what happens when
I do that instead?

With so much humility and vulnerability,
I began doing and saying things
I never thought I was capable of,
or previously even wanted to do.

Each time I chose a new adventure
I would get very quiet
and feel into my body to feel what I felt:
peace or tension?
soothed or activated?
calm or reactive?

With every scenario
or touchy pokey moment
I learned more than half
my instinctive responses to other people
were driven by self-protection.

I could see and feel clearly for the first time:
When I wanted to run,
When I wanted to hide,
When I wanted to shut down,

When I wanted to lash out,
When I wanted to scream and yell,
When I wanted to make myself small.

And the other half ...
the whispers,
the murmurs,
the "oh this just doesn't sit right"
was my soul.

Always there,
but easy to ignore
under the old alarm bells.

My body was always giving me
the guidance
but it was so very quiet
I had never heard it before.

This was the magic delivered to me,
by giving myself permission
to believe my thinking was total shit.

By listening to my body,
I found an entirely new way of being.

"We cannot solve our problems with
the same thinking we used
when we created them."
Brilliance we've heard before from Mr. Einstein,

My sweet loves,
if you truly desire change,
if you want to experience
what you've never had before,
give yourself permission
to believe your thinking
is absolute, utter trash.

Give yourself permission to go slow.

And listen to the wisdom
that calmly sits in your body.

Create the space
for a new way of being
to bubble up to the surface.

And when you do,
act with courage and bravery,
often some humility and vulnerability
to do the things you never
knew you could.

It's freeing.
And a radical act of self trust
and transformation.

It's there whenever you are ready.

UNBECOMING

I realized that I've spent
the last ten years unbecoming me.

Knowing she is nothing more
than a refractory of all the millions
of perceptions and masks,
reflections and layers
of my life lived.

An amalgamation of what
has occurred in my life
until today.

And she does not exist.
The more we own who we are,
the more we solidify a construct
that isn't real to begin with.
You are not your identity.

Because who you are is soul.

And soul is the essence of consciousness
imbued in your physical body.

And we are all made of the same stuff,
stardusts and galaxies gone by,
mixed with an intelligence far beyond
our comprehension.

And...
Matter is Love.

We are literally made of the frequency
of the vibration of what we call love.

So love, my darling dear friends,
is not an action.

It's not what we do.
It is what we are.

And it's not just us.
Everything,
every single thing that is matter,
is love.

We live in love on the daily.

If we pull these concepts together,
what we come to accept is
the personalities, quirks, traits,
image of our identity mixed
with some ego for fun
makes it nearly impossible
to live in our bodies.

So we hide in our mind
and our thoughts,
where we can make
these illusions seem real.

When we live in the body,
we must confront
that this fake reality actually hurts us,
not helps us,
even though it seems easier.

This is why most healing journeys
involve a heaping dose of pain
and liberating trauma from the body.

Spiritual folk call them dark nights of the soul.

Because living from

the false cocoon of our mind,
is what drives our belief
that we are separate
from each other
and separate from truest nature,
capital L, Love.

The more we identify with our thoughts
and our sense of self,
the more disconnected we will feel.

And we struggle.
And we hurt.

The more quickly you let go
of who you think you are
and how you've made it through
the world this far
and the layers of identity
which are nothing more than
layers of conditioning from past hurts,
and patterns of being to keep you safe,
the more you are able to liberate your soul
and live in love.

Wild, huh?

So maybe, just maybe,
take the plunge
and allow your sense of self
to soften around the edges
and release reality from your thoughts.

Sink slowly,
more deeply into your body.
Feel the truth of who you are
and know that you are Love.

I promise your heart has never forgotten.

BE A LADY

I used to pee with the faucet running.

I envied women on movie screens
who could be effortlessly naked
in romantic trysts.

I couldn't stand the sight of my naked self,
let alone anyone seeing me.

There was an inherent
wrongness to my body,
simply for being a body.

Its appearance
and
its function.

To grow up meant I was to transcend
its animal qualities,
biological nature.

Be a lady,
not a beast of flesh and bone.

It was the intensity of this belief,
my body was repulsive,
that led me to a place in which
the very nature of my body's expression
was mortifying.
Poop, Pee, Periods.
Vile.
Disgusting.
Unforgivable.

I operated in a constant state

of disdain and denial.

Hide any evidence of my body's function.
And secretly hate myself for having a body at all.

With this adversarial approach
to my body,
I led crusades in starvation.

Cruelly punished me
with binging and purging.
Exercised manically.
Or not at all for months.
Or drowned it out with booze.

And ignored any possible sensation
or feedback my body was giving me.

Recoiled from and was irritated it would
communicate back to me.

Seethed that it would continue
to remind me it was there.

When my frustration grew too much,
I whaled my fists into my stomach,
my sides, and my thighs until bruises
spidered across my skin.

"You are disgusting."
"I hate you."
"No one will love you."

Only I did not love me.

This was my shame.

Brené says, shame is
"the intense painful feeling

or experience of believing
we are flawed
and therefore unworthy
of acceptance and belonging."

I could not hate myself
anymore for being human.

Fundamentally flawed.
Irrevocably unworthy.

The sticky point about shame
is that we believe no one else
feels the shame that we feel.

That we are alone.
Isolated.
The other.
This is what allows shame to
thrive and survive.

I may not feel shame about the
same things you feel shame about.
But I felt shame burn me up
from the inside out.

And sometimes still do.

Shame needs the dark
recesses of our mind.

Our pathway through is to
shine a light on it.

Shine, my loves, shine.

MOTHERING

I never wanted to be a mother.

In fact, I told my ex-husband
if he ever wanted kids, to get married,
or some other fairytale life bullshit,
it would never be me.

I was convinced that I didn't have
what it took to be a good mother.

No maternal instinct.

I wasn't kind enough.
Or soft enough.
Or nurturing enough.

I just didn't know what to do with babies
who wiggled and fussed and needed me.

How would I ever know what to give them?

It's silly now when I think of this fear.

Because from the moment
I was on two feet,
I was with my animals.
Dogs, cats, eventually horses.
Doting on them all.

Watching tiny micro-changes in their expressions,
anticipating their needs,
and snuggling with them for hours.

Petting their faces,
soothing them,

feeding them,
grooming them,
singing to them,
and playing with them.

I received too little
of this soothing, comforting, and care
and so I wore the mantle
of what I was given
as who I was.

This is the way
we take on the trauma
of generations before us
and believe it is who we are.

It's not.

And if we don't examine this closely,
these embedded beliefs
that were given to us in the ways
we were treated,
will be what we pass along in our children.

Now I see so clearly,
I've mothered every living being
that has crossed my path.

And mothering my children
has become my most holy work,
dismantling as many falsehoods as I can
to not taint them with our collective past.

And mothering myself.
Rocking and tending
to each piece of myself
that was not loved through,
accepted, and protected.

I have always been a mother.
And a good one at that.

Remember, my loves,
how you were treated
is not who you are.

Just because you weren't given it,
doesn't mean you don't have it
in your blood.

Be what is most natural in your soul,
not who you were conditioned to be.

That is your honest liberation.

WILD WOMEN SPEAK

I was ten or eleven
and was so frustrated
rolling with anger
all I could do was run.

I walked out the front door
no shoes on my feet
ran through one yard and the next
until I made it to the edge of two fields
with a dirt track between them.

I ran with all the force my body could find.

I ran until my lungs seized
and pushed harder
collapsing, hands on knees,
adrenaline pumping through my blood
and snatched for air
the moment I had enough.

I turned and ran home
pushing my legs harder
driving my toes deeper into soft black earth
my mind emptied from my anger.

I used to romanticize this moment
as an sign of my love for running.

Almost like it was born in me this need to run.
I realize now this was the only pathway
I had to express my anger and frustration.

It wasn't safe to say what my body
needed saying with my words.

As a small child I could only run it out in a
self-punishing way.

And it was the only way I could
find freedom in my oppression.
The flight part of fight or flight
because I could not fight
and release this emotion trapped within me.

Now as I dream what year 39 will be I tell myself:

No more shrinking
No more minimizing
No more self-punishing and self-abandoning
No more dimming
No more editing and perfecting
No more picking battles
No more choosing the right time
No more centering others comfort or egos
above my own expression, needs, and safety.

Because now what I know
is those nasty women who are
wild, unruly, untamed
are just women with big spirits
and big voices
who say the unpopular things
and voice their disagreements
and illuminate mistreatments and injustices
at the risk of being labeled difficult.

Unliked and unpopular.

These are the women who run with wolves
as Dr. Pinkola Estes taught us in the stories
of Baba Yaga and the rest.

They were not evil or wicked
but they were feared

because they exposed
all the things others wanted to keep hidden.

To remain in control
and these women
were absolutely uncontrollable.

Remember this, my loves,
true power is self expression.

Never shy away from that power.

Stand in your power
and say all the things
even when your voice shakes.

BENEATH THE MASK

For most of my life,
I've been a social chameleon.

Due to a highly attuned nervous system
thanks to relational trauma,
I'm incredibly perceptive
of small nonverbal cues that give me
some insight into how others are receiving me.

We say things colloquially like,
"I'm empathic" or
"I can read people really well" or
"I'm intuitive."

I use this highly refined ability
to people-please.
The response is called fawning.

And it can be one of our first activations
of our sympathetic nervous system
known as our social engagement system
when we feel our connection to another
as uncertain or unsafe.

While I often seem very much myself
in person or social media,
willing to stand out or be rebellious,
often enjoying a little limelight,
it is rarely unguarded.
It's measured,
sometimes, calculated.

And there is no mistaking why
I've preferred the medium of writing,
which gives me complete control

over every word choice.

This is one of the pieces
I struggle with most in myself.

A blessing and a curse.

I'm a fantastic plus one at any wedding,
I will make friends wherever I go,
and fit in with anyone
and have a conversation about anything.

And yet, I have to consciously challenge
myself to be truly vulnerable.

Open.
Transparent.

To speak or be seen in a way
that I can sense will not be well-received
but is honest.

It is one of the scariest fucking things I have ever done.

Worse yet, there is often a deep longing
to be really seen as I am
and often, unsure if others see me
or the mask I've intentionally
or unintentionally created.

The only antidote I know is connection.

When my beating heart attunes to yours.

When I feel the vibration and frequency
that melts like warmth
all through my chest and soft core,
my careful words stop.

My masks fall.
This sense of safety that stops time.
We are connected.

And it no longer matters
what I think
or what you think.

Peace in what is shared
between us
in this moment.

This is the truth that transmutes our fears.

Connection
between
my body
and yours,
my heart
and yours,
my soul
and yours.

WHAT I CAME HERE TO BE

My dad gave me an army green plastic bin
that held hundreds of
National Geographic animal cards.

A beautiful picture matched
with facts like diet,
lifespan, habitat etc.
He used to quiz me on them
and how animals moved together.

Geese? Gaggle
Lions? Pride
Fish? School
Crows? Murder
Dolphins? Pod

I would sit with those cards
alone on the cold, concrete driveway,
singing songs to myself for hours,
imagining myself an animal
just like them
at play in the wild.

I look back on my child self
and see innocence naturally,
but also open-hearted imagination.

I understood the brutality of nature,
but when I watched nature programs
on PBS with my dad,
I would always squeal
and yell at the tv
when the cheetah caught the gazelle.

My dad would tell me,

"Ashley, it's nature.
The Cheetah would die if it
didn't eat the Gazelle."

There were a lot of lessons
I learned as I grew up
and that innocence left me.

"Be more realistic."
"Be more practical."
"That's not the way the world works."

I started to learn that
there wasn't just
predators and prey on the savannah,
but also that there
might be predators
who would eagerly
take advantage of a child, teen,
young woman as doe-eyed
and naive as me.

The message was clear:
"Get tough, kid. Grow a thicker skin
or you are going to be eaten alive out there."

So I did.

I became suspicious,
clever, stealthy,
and learned to move
like a Jaguar.

Hide my heart,
hide my innocence,
hide my awe,
hide the best parts of me.

And the pendulum swung

from Pollyanna
to stone-cold cynic.

No one was going to get anything past me.
Chain smoking and sarcastic.

But all that I received
when I hardened myself
to the world
was a very practical, realistic,
kill-or-be-killed life
that was brutal
and cruel to me.

And that is not at all
what I came here
to be,
live,
or do.
I want fucking magic.
I want joy and BLISS.

I want miracles
and life that is the unfolding
its own great fairytale.

My greatest work has been
to return to a life of joy
after living in so many years of struggle,
hard fighting for everything I had,
protecting myself from the cruel world.

Dissolving the walls
that became my very own cage,
looking for predators everywhere.

I find now the more I play with life,
life plays with me in co-creation
with flow and ease.

Blinking open again my eyes
to see as a child
in delight and wonder.

Opening my heart
to let love flow through,
singing sweet songs of peace
to myself once more.

And I welcome a life
of limitless possibilities
and infinite opportunities.

Mystery and Magic.
Unexplained and ever so juicy and delicious.
A witness to my life as my own miracle.

And you can have this experience too, my love.
It's yours.

THE WARRIOR'S HEART

"I will never wave the white flag of my surrender!"

A declaration I proudly believed
was the source of my strength.

I'll fight it out.

Tenacious.
Tough.
Fucking gritty.

I'll use every ounce of juice in my body to avoid
surrendering to circumstances that suck.

Until situations, people,
and experiences just got harder.

Things became insurmountable.

No matter how much energy
and power I tapped,
I could not win.

The struggle was real.

In more than a few moments in my life,
I have dropped to my knees in tears
begging for grace.

Pleading for my peace and the will to
make it through my suffering.

The answer is clear: stop fighting.

Surrender.

When I deeply surrender to my suffering,
to what is in this moment,
I am free.

I'm cleansed in my heart
with a unending peace
that makes way for waves of bliss
as I finally taste liberation.

It never comes from the fight.
It always comes when
I cannot fight anymore.

Surrender is the bravest action
I ever take in my suffering.

Surrender is the embodiment
of immovable trust in this life
of mine and me.

Surrender is not weakness, my love.
It is the courage of your warrior heart at its fiercest.

Surrender the fight.
Surrender in love.

THE HUNTER'S STARS

I have a very weird allergy to deer,
not the meat but the hide.

You would think it would be hard
to discover this or easy to avoid,
but my dad was an avid hunter,
and growing up he processed in the garage,
and butchered in the kitchen.

What started as itchy, puffy eyes
eventually progressed
to itchy, scratchy throats and difficulty breathing.

The last night my dad ever butchered
at our house,
I had such a severe reaction
that my entire face and jaw
puffed in hives and I struggled to breathe.

My dad took me for a walk after 11:30
on a particularly icy and crisp November night.

My parents house was the last in the row
and after we walked past our tree line,
we were engulfed in an endless black sky
under countless shining stars.

We walked and he talked to me
about each constellation
he could find in the sky,
distracting me from my wheezy breathing
and cold fingers.

He pointed out the standards
like the big and little dippers,

pointing to the North Star,
and then he told me about Orion,
the great hunter, with the sister stars
that line his belt as he pulled back
his eternal bow strings.

It is one of my favorite memories.

Since this night, anytime I see the stars,
I look for Orion as he moves
from horizon to center stage
in the night sky.

I tell my kids about him and they act
like I'm silly to be so excited
to see the hunter again.

This is a piece of my joy,
my heart,
for over twenty years.

When I think about this moment,
it came from a night that was not
intentionally special.

Actually, it was rather scary to begin,
but the total presence of being with my dad
and seeing the stars twinkly alive
became magic to me
that forever lives in my body.

This is where our joy lives.

In the every day ordinary
in our true presence.

And often we are distracted and busy,
with phones in front of our faces,
rushing from one thing to the next,

we settle for fleeting happiness
rather than endless joy.

Be here now, my loves.

As I stepped out on my front porch
at 5:40 this morning,
I saw Orion the Hunter watching over me,
and thought of writing you
so you may feel again the joys
from ordinary moments in your childhood
that still live with you today.

STAND IN THE SUN

I was isolated in this last year.

Every single relationship I counted on
Every friendship
Every family connection
Every romantic connection
Every business connection
That I trusted
Started breaking away in 2022,
Dissolved in 2023.

Culminating with nearly dying on 2/24/24.

And the one thing I know
is that it forced me to swirl around
in my darkness.

Deep.

Exactly what I needed.
Confronting every aspect that was shamed.
Blamed.
Rejected.
Repressed.
Hated.
Shunned.

And the most haunting truth
I danced with in myself
was that there was nothing more
to cut away.

I could not bear to try
to mold myself even more to fit in.

Healing is not repairing broken parts of ourselves.

Healing is loving,
accepting and honoring the parts
that were silenced,
that we now fear to shed light on.

Authentically being your whole self,
not minimizing anything,
is love.

The truth is that most pain we encounter
from the time we are children on
as we are belittled and criticized
is the parts in ourselves
that others are unwilling
to accept in themselves.

It's compounded because
those in positional power
diminish power in another
to remain in control.

They leverage their control
to meet their needs
or exploit situations for their benefit
when love is absent
and fear is driving behavior.

Those of us who dim our light
to keep the peace
and smooth the feathers
end up silencing whole chunks of ourselves away
to try to keep everyone else happy.

What I have found is
unconditional love for every part of me
is freedom.

And I love you the same.

Unconditionally.
Wholly.
Shadow and light.

But I will never surround myself again
with those who do not walk in
their own authenticity.

Those who have not begun to love themselves wholly.

Those who are still tripping through
facades of ego,
grappling with power and status.

These are the ones who are dangerous.
And as I have learned,
they may be happy to let you die.
Nah. No, thanks.
I'll pass on that.

Joy
Peace
Bliss

are only found in the complete, true, whole self.
Messy, wild, fierce, and free.

And as these chapters end,
new chapters begin.

You are perfectly imperfect
in service to this world.

Join me, babes, because
I love all of you unconditionally
and it's time to stand in the sun.

PART II: LET YOURSELF BE SWALLOWED WHOLE

"In the depth of winter, I finally learned that within me there lay an invincible summer." Albert Camus

LET YOURSELF BE SWALLOWED WHOLE

I used to be terrified of feeling hungry.
Seems silly.

But the sensation of an empty stomach
would send ripples of anxiety through my body.
Sometimes, sheer panic.

Because of my disordered eating,
hunger was one of the
most dangerous things I could feel.

Because when I was hungry,
I would make "bad" choices.

I would be overwhelmed by my hunger
and would choose the pizza,
burger, fries, fast food drive thru.

When I was hungry, I'd lost control.

I lived much of my 20s doing anything
I could to prevent myself from ever feeling hunger.
I snacked a lot.
Smoked cigarettes to curb food cravings.

My next meal was always on my mind.
And the mental math of how much
and when and what I could
eat was an ever-present calculation.

As I mended my relationship with my body,
I realized a couple things...

Hunger wasn't the only thing I was afraid of.

I was deeply afraid of my body
and the myriad of sensations
it was always sending me.

I was deeply afraid of my feelings,
my emotions, too.
Afraid of being overwhelmed by them.
Swallowed whole.

That if I let myself feel everything,
I would have to feel the deep ache
of a longing that never stopped.

It penetrated to the core of me,
and to feel that longing,
unleashed an unending sadness in me.

I realized that I numbed my feelings
of hunger by constantly staying full
and I numbed my feelings of my longing
by constantly staying distracted.

I spent an entire summer a few years back
making peace with my hunger.
Counter to what any modern-day
eating disorder clinic would advocate,
I allowed myself to swing the pendulum
from constant grazing to extended periods,
hours not days, of not eating,
and eating much less
but nutrient-dense and plant-based,
not low-cal starvation.

It was through allowing myself
to sink deeply into hunger,
let it swallow me up,
I stayed steady in it.

Feeling the pit in my stomach growl

that I found peace in the ache
of an empty belly.

Learned to breathe while
I felt every hunger pain.

I didn't abandon myself or retreat,
or try to fix or soothe.

I just allowed everything I was feeling to be.

And I reset myself in
my attuned listening to my body
to follow its actual biological cues for hunger
instead of my fight or flight response
and mind's anxiety.

I see the same as being true
for my own self growth work today
with all the rest of my feeling and sensations.

I open to them, instead of push them away.
Let them crash into me.
Drown me if they must.

Widen the path of my experience
deeper into me
and just as I discovered with
my sensations of hunger,
my longing, my feelings, my desires,
my aches for wholeness,
can be ever-present,
and yet, I'm still okay.

I'm still fine.
I'm still safe.

Beneath all this whirring
of being a human

alive in a very sensitive body,
I'm still love at my core.

So are you.

My invitation for you is
to consider where you may reject
your feelings and sensations
out of fear of being overwhelmed by them.

And maybe just maybe,
let yourself be swallowed whole.

So you can see as I have
that when the waves stop crashing,
you're still there.

Safe and Loved.

I AM NOT A GOOD PERSON

We are our best in the world
when we have
no self
to believe in.

When there is nothing
and no one
to identify with.

I'm not a good person.
a kind person.
a wise person.
nor a successful person either.

And the opposite is equally true.

I'm not a bad person.
a cruel person.
a foolish person.
a lazy bump on a log person.

I am.

What remains is far more important
once we drop the self,
we make way for soul to emerge.

Our soul comes packed
with our unique gifts,
the birth of creativity and innovation,
and guiding principles to live by.

These principles will challenge us
to meet the highest bar, standard,

exemplary ideal of the best kind of human,
and the more you live from your soul,
you will be that in everything you do.

No self required.

You will just be,
and become.

And life is juicy,
passionate, magical,
and deeply loving.

But this is hard to do.

It requires courage, and discipline,
and awareness of our thoughts,
feelings, and internal experiences,
and a keen awareness of others as well.

Most of the time it requires an ever-present
holding of the tension of opposites,
and the ability to move through our lives
very slowly,
and pay close attention to
what is unfolding in this moment.

Erupting forth is an unshakable authenticity
that is palpable,
and powerful,
magnetic,
trustworthy,
and true.

This is the work.

Not in carving our "selfs" up.
Trying to cut out an aspect
of our self that does not match

who we think we should be.

No. This is a fool's errand.
And a waste of our precious life force.

It is eliminating the desire to mold,
hone or shape,
hide or highlight aspects of the self at all.

Instead focus your effort
on uncovering your standard
that your soul holds as your true north
and pursue that standard
again and again
on your worst day
and your best day.

Realigned to hold a vision of the world
that matches the beauty,
dignity and integrity of what it means
to be guided by divine grace
and Gaia's wisdom,
and surrendering anything that is not that,
including who I like to think I am.

THE DANCE OF DARKNESS AND LIGHT

Days like today I understand how the witch
decided to eat Hansel and Gretel.

How Baba Yaga eats babies.
How Hecate let blood.
How Circe poisoned men.
How Kali Ma severed heads,
waving her swords in her many arms.
How Sekhmet with the head of a lioness
savagely ripped anyone in her path apart.

Today, I feel the fierce rumble shake
through my thighs and
run heat up my spine.

It says, "Try me..."

It shakes me to my core,
thrilling and uneasy.

The darkness of the sacral elements
of our feminine energy are destructive,
terrifying, brutal and relentless,
just like the fierceness present in Mother Nature.

Our culture has denied
what once was revered,
honored, and respected...
the depth of our human darkness.

Now, we hide behind bullshit love
and light sentiments.
High vibes only.

The more we deny ourselves

the much needed passages
into the underworld,
our dark nights of the soul,
guided only by our intuition
and the moon,
the more we take away
the ability to heal and transform,
and this fiery power of transformation stifled
will lead us astray,
and our fury will come out side ways.

Fights with our people.
Self Destructive behavior
like binge eating or drinking.
Rash decisions that only
create more heartache and difficulty.

No, my loves.

We need to whisper to
the dark goddess in each of us.

Court her.
Love her.
Let her primal drive surface again and again.
Be held in the shadows,
and coaxed to purr in the light.

Every single one of these goddesses
are the rulers of
death and destruction
atrocity and war
and they are the rulers of
healing and prosperity,
birth and fertility.

We can't have one without the other.

We can only hold compassion

for another's suffering and intense pain
when we've met our own.

We must forge and burn through
our lowest base desires
in the fires of our intense longing
to awaken the magic
of healing and divinity.

They are one.

Shakti destroys and delights.
She dances in both realms.

So do you, mama.

Feel her.
Breathe fire.

Heal your heart
and crack it
wide open to the sky
in all your primal power
so you may rise renewed.

BURN THE LEDGERS

One of the greatest heartaches I've witnessed
is our transactional state
of perceiving each other.

We've simplified our experiences down
to an endless strings of if/then dichotomies.

We've limited every action
and every function
into a desired outcome
to maximize efficiency
and productivity.
And while this is a potent method for achievement,
we've grown wearily impatient
with one another and our lives.

I did it. I did the thing, gimme my result.

I see it in relationships most of all.

I was nice to you,
be nice to me.

I did you a favor,
do me one in return.

I love you.
Love me back.

We've normalized this shorthand
for back-scratching reciprocity
that amounts nothing more
to an endless game of keeping score.

Those who seem to keep the ledger balanced

are more worthy of our efforts.

Yet, this is woefully inadequate.

First of all, it limits our worthiness
of a life of love and bliss down
to our ability to continuously
do things for each other.

If I'm not in a constant state of doing
and over-giving,
and pleasing,
and managing everyone else's experience,
how will I ever get mine?

This is fucking trash.
Plus, it breeds unworthiness,
low self-esteem and devaluing
of what it means to be human.

I promise you, my love,
if you never did another thing in this world,
you would still be the most magnificent creature
worthy of juicy, soul-stirring devotion
and magics untold.

And more, we lose the polished beauty
in consistent effort that has yet-to-yield results.
To toil with no thought of harvest.

Because is not the achievement
of the result that changes us,
but its pursuit.

And in this way we fail to use our lives,
our relationships, our work,
like small passes of sandpaper
gently wearing away
at our more jagged edges

because it doesn't give us
fast-food instant satisfaction.

So darling, I beg you, burn the ledgers.
Stop tallying the score.

Let go of any belief that asks you
to boil down your being
to the immediate gratification
of what you can get done today
and who you can do it for.

Be in this moment fully,
working for a future you've yet to meet,
you've yet to dream into existence,
and love with no expectation of return.
Be ever so fucking gritty in your persistence
of being all of you in every way,
in every relationship,
all of the time.

You will be endlessly pleased with the results.

ANGER SPEAKS

I love my anger.

For most of my life
I thought it was my biggest flaw.

A quick mind and cutting tongue
meant that in explosions of my anger
I would lash out and cruelly hurt
those I loved most.

I spent years trying to calm
the fire in my belly.

I bit my tongue
I walked away
I shamed myself relentlessly
for being a hot head.

Wild and uncivilized
A loose cannon
Or as one boss called me,
"A rabid pitbull."

Fuck, huh?

And then I stopped fighting her.
I slowed down long enough
to listen to what
she was trying to tell me.

And I realized that my anger
wasn't the worst part of me.

My anger was the part of me
that always had my own back

that protected me time and time again,
when I was being mistreated,
taken advantage of,
disregarded or degraded.

My anger knew every single time
that this was fucking bullshit.

Now, I love her.

I feel her roll through me
like a hot electric storm
racing across prairie.

She is keen and wise
and ever so perceptive
with a power that will split the skies.

I refuse to ask her to be less.
But I don't often allow her center stage.

She doesn't get to speak for me any longer.
She is a only a guide.
One of my most trusted.

And with her by my side,
I now know exactly when to have a boundary,
say no,
advocate for more,
and politely excuse myself
from people, places or spaces
that may wish to do me harm.

No, thank you. I'm out.

The only time I let her off the leash now
is when someone fucks with my people.

Try it...

The trick to this magical experience
of living this life of ours
is to stop cutting away
the slices and slivers of ourselves
that have every right to be there.

Letting go of our disgust and shame
for our pokey bits,
our wildness,
our impolite
or messy bits.

Instead, we must meet them,
understand them, and love them.

Anytime we try to remove them,
we are committing violence against ourselves.

Love is nothing more than
radical self acceptance.

Be all of who you are, mamas.

You are fucking brilliant.

Be you in love
with all your fire
and all your power

A FIERCE RETURN TO MYSELF

When I was 21
at a popular downtown bar
blitzed out of my mind
I ran into a group of guys I knew
and considered friends.

They could see I was trashed
and it was bar close
so they offered to let me crash at their house
and sleep it off
rather than try to make it home alone.

Through cuts and splices
I have shards of memories
... driving home
... face against a cold backseat window
... stumbling into a kitchen
... arms around the waist of one of the guys
... a blurry guy sitting at the kitchen table
... laughs and jokes
... having trouble with my shoes
... beers cracking open
and then nothing.

Black.

Silence.

Until I came to
that morning with this guy
on top of me
only to realize
we were having sex
except it wasn't sex
because there was no consent

57

and I knew him.

I trusted him to get me home safely.

Incoherent and drunk still,
I closed my eyes
blacked out again
and woke up alone,
sick,
in the bed
found my clothes
in a pile on the floor
and I left
saw no one as I slipped
back through the kitchen.

I didn't tell a soul.

I wanted to bury
every fragment of that night
far down in my body
down in the dark
knowing what happened felt wrong
but confused if it was my fault
and having no idea
of what actually happened
while totally blacked out.

It wasn't until my early 30s
that I understood the gravity
and trauma of what happened to me.

It wasn't until I was
sexually assaulted a second time
did I begin to unearth
these old college memories
I had cleverly forgotten.

I began to hold myself in such a way

that I absolutely knew
I didn't deserve these things
that I wasn't to blame
it wasn't my fault.

And I was fucking angry.

Fuck these guys that I trusted.

Now years later, as I date in my late 30s
and I experience waves of panic
and often want to blame myself
when I become uncomfortable,
uncertain, afraid, and I dip out...
a vicious voice loves saying,
"what the fuck, Ash.
why do you keep doing this?"

And then I remember
because I am learning to simultaneously

... trust myself in an entirely new way
... believe in my intuition first
... heal myself and my body
... and learn to trust someone new
all at the same time
taking a tremendous leap of faith
every time I sit across the table
on a first date that I will be ok.

It is fucking hard work.

And yet, the pieces of me
I've reclaimed
feel like liberation.
Like breathing new air.

Unending waves of grace
and compassion I continue to find for myself

and such a visceral, fierce power
that I almost lost
rises again in me
more solid in knowing
exactly what is for me
and what is not.

This truth is white hot.

And even when I am scared this work
to slowly feel everything
my body has to offer
shaky breathing,
racing heart,
and gently nurture myself when I am hurting
sets me free.

To be with me no matter what comes up
and have the courage to keep going
and try to vulnerably explain it when I can,
this is unconditional love for myself.

So this is what I know:
Do the work, my loves.

Even when its hard.

You are brave.
And you are strong.

If I can do it,
so can you.

SCARRED HEARTS, MORE LOVE

What we don't want to hear
about how we live in the world
with others ...

It's not the cold words you spoke to me,
the thoughtless or selfish actions
I perceived or felt,
its the feeling of loss and separation
that I've lived a million times
before this moment.

This is what fucks us up.

This is why we get stuck
and are unable to move through
and heal...
those millions of memories
embedded in every cell of our being.

But we don't see that.

Instead we blame
the other person right there
in front of us
with the pokey words and actions.

Fuck you for saying that.
Fuck you for doing that.

You can't treat me that way.

And we push back hard.
Lash out, offer cruelty back.

Or as I often do,

shut down.
Disappear.
Cut bait and run,
long and far away.

No one gets out of this lifetime unscathed.

By the time we are in
our 20s, 30s, 40s and beyond,
we are carrying lifetimes
of wounds on our heavy hearts.

But usually its a handful of experiences
in our earliest days that slice the first cut
in our tender soft hearts
that teach us falsely
that we have to perform for or earn love.

So we learn to cope
by either doing anything to keep
the fleeting false conditional love
we so desire safe
or we learn to be okay alone
denying our deepest desires and needs.

And from that moment on
it is the trauma of re-experiencing situations
that mirror that first wound
that we live again
and again
and again.

The deepest healing comes
when we stop demanding others treat us
in a way that doesn't expose us
to scars we are protecting,
but instead when we can honor
that each poke and paper cut
has absolutely nothing to do

with the person standing in front of us.

And everything to do with
holding our own hearts so gently
we can find safety in letting others in
and feel with every bit of our being
that what connects you to me,
scarred heart to scarred heart,
is unconditional love
that never stops
never ceases
and is our natural state of being.

This is the work, my loves.

Not to find the right person.
Not to ask others to jump through hoops.

But to be so soft and patient
with one another
that we allow every ache
to become a moment
to offer grace to one another
and ourselves.

This is how we heal old scars and ancient pains.
Through the ever present loving
and care for ourselves and each other.

Again and again until the end of time.

THE TRUTH WITHIN

There is a difference between
expressing emotions
and expressing truth.

As a verbal child
and a deeply feeling being,
since I was young
I could always tell you
what I felt.

As my friends tell me to this day,
"Ashley, your face is being very loud."

Expression has never been my problem.

Knowing what I'm feeling
has never been the issue.

Expressing my truth now...

Not my idea.
Not my knowledge.
Not my education.

But my truth is altogether different.

The kind of truth
that sends electricity
out into the ether
and reverberates
into your cells
like deep low notes
plucked on an earthy cello.

The kind of truth that

shivers and shakes
as it leaves my throat,
breathy and soaked with my soul.

To breathe life into this truth
and let it leave my body
is the form of intimacy
that for the longest time
terrified me most.

The kind that gives voice
to the purest parts
of my heart
through my entire body.

That leaves me full seen through.

Raw
Naked
Exposed

Yet over this last year,
my fear of my truth began to lose its grip.

It grimaced, snarled,
and tried to cling.
Demanding that no one see,
or feel,
or know my truth,
just water it down
and make it more acceptable.

But my truth began to roll
in my belly with a ferocity
I could not tame.

And shook me free of my fear
to stand in faith.

As my truth began to roll from my lips,
my illusions were shattered.

Because with every drop
of my whole self
I know that living
in my truth,
rich, soul-soaked truth,
is the only path to liberation.

So maybe there is nothing.
Just being.
With my truth.
My heart.
And you.

Speak loudly, clearly, and boldly, my loves.

THE BRAVERY OF AN OPEN HEART

I want to turn away from the cold.
I want to insulate my heart from hurt.
I want to deny the ache that feels unmet.

And yet in any of these actions,
this hiding, running, erecting towers
to hide my heart away
like princesses in fairytales
is not the answer.

My superpower is
not my strength in shielding
my heart from hurt.

My superpower is to open more fiercely each time,
leaning in and loving more deeply and openly.

To the deepest depths of the ocean.

This is the power and intensity of the feminine.

Opening again to the depths
of my own heartache
and heartbreak
and returning to love again
has become my greatest truth.

When I can feel tenderly into the pieces of me
that want to steal my heart,
to open myself to the ravishment
of everything this earthly experience has to offer,
to return to love again,
and again.

To make space with all that I am,

and allow me to share that love
simply, easily, and freely,
then and only then
am I free.

To love unconditionally is not a foolish quest.
It is the bravest one I know.

THE ALCHEMY OF GOING DEEPER

I started writing to sell you things.

And then I learned the power of story,
and I used my life to sell you things.

I wrote about alotta embarrassing things.
A tide swelled up into my throat
and writing my stories became catharsis,
not just sales.

Later it became metamorphosis
as I learned to share my tangled experience
of being in my body heavy with ugliness in me
that I once tried to hide from the light.

Eating disorders, my self-hatred,
my numbing with booze and
complicated feelings about marriage
and mothering.

I laid open as much as I dared each day
often feeling sick as I clicked post
and walking away for hours to avoid
seeing how you received my words.

It became my medicine.

I forced myself in such a way
you could feel my heart and
with each word you read
hoped you would know
you are not alone.

And 2021 found me with alchemy.

Turns out the last five years
of bringing my stories to the surface
was just the warm up round.

Fuckkkkkkk.

Through writing I located those hurts
and acknowledged them,
sharing them with the world.

And that was the fucking easy part.

Because what came next
was to live that pain again.
To drown deeply in it.
To stop finding it
and now be it.

To willingly allow that pain to alchemize
and never again leave me the same person
I once was.

Utter annihilation of who I knew
and the life I led for 36 years.

Now deeper than any pit of pain
I felt in my lowest rock bottom points
because those rock bottom days
were still about avoiding my feelings,
avoiding my heart ...
I rode a roller coaster,
plunging into my pain
but it was no longer driven by stories of my mind,
it was reliving it through my body.

Days of sorrow that broke over me,
breaking through me.
Followed by days of unsurpassed joy.
Lightness returned to me every time

I dipped into my darkness.

I wasn't just free in my mind,
now, free in my body.

The truth is ascension is not reaching
for the light, elevating, or vibrating higher,
it's learning that the light
is only found in the dark.

It's immersing deeper and deeper
into the unknown only to find that
when you break on the surface for air
that the entire world has changed.

You have changed.
You are irrevocably different.
Blinking above in the light with new eyes.

I lost a lifetime of memories.
Barely remember who I was
how I talked
or what I believed.

She's just gone.
In her place is a power and peace
that I have never known.

I broke myself only to find out I can't be broken.

And now blessed with waves
of bliss to be alive in this body,
giving meaning to every moment,
in a life that is by any standard meaningless
in the big scheme of things.

And all my heart can do is dance in this discovery.

If you are brave,

do the same.
The body is the path.

It's never been your mind and mindset.
That's just the warm-up round, baby.

Go deep.

You'll never be the same again.
I promise with all my heart.

PART III: SACRED WORK

"The body never lies." Martha Graham

SACRED WORK

Broken people don't
know they are broken.

They think this is just the way life is.
And they roll through people
like a wave of chaos and destruction.

Broken people will destroy
everything sweet
in their lives because
all they know is breaking things.

Healing people, though,
they know they are hurting.
Because when you hurt
you know intuitively that
there must be something more
beyond the hurt.

The hurt brings hope that
the hurting will end.
And when you feel
how bad that hurt burns,
you heal.

And as you heal your hurts,
you know and feel hurting
when you see it in others.

You see how hurting connects us
all in the same suffering,
no matter how your separate wounds look.
They all bleed the same..

Hurting people are the holy people among us.

And hurting heal themselves
by holding their hurts.
And healers heal the hurting
by holding their hearts.
And this is holy work.

The place of the sacred wound that connects us all.

Oh, and the broken, they are not so bad.
They are only unable to feel
the searing pain of their hurts just yet.
They are numb to themselves.

And so to these hearts
we offer compassion.

Because the broken do not
believe they are worthy of
the sweetness of life and love
they so desperately deserve.

But one day, the broken will feel
the breaking of their hearts.

They'll become the hurting,
and then
the healing,
holy too.

To be alive is sacred work.

Do not ever forget this.

HEART'S TRUTH

I want to turn away some days.

Silently slip back into the
hum of every day
filled with busyness and to-dos.

This journey is long.
And in my weary frustration
I want to quit.
Give up.

And yet, my heart cries out to me,
"I'm still here!"

And I can feel her truth.
The knowing that is deep
and shakes my whole being.

She says, "this is the way!"

And I know that I must follow.
Because it is the path written
in the stars and carved in my being.

There is no other way worth going.
I must go where she leads.

Even when the way
becomes hard to find,
and longer than I think I can endure.

With hand over my heart,
pulling one deep breath
after the next into my little body,
rest for a moment,

and on we go.

With faith found once more,
renewed with a strength that says,
"one more day."

My heart,
your heart,
will not lead us astray.

Keep going.

THE ESSENCE OF US

Unconditional love is far simpler
than we give it credit for.

It's not passion or blossoming romance.
It's not deep devotion,
or care, adoration, and affection.

It's being.
Simple being.

That is unconditional love.
The essence of our truest nature.

It is cracking ourselves wide open
to be before each other
who are in the same state as ourselves,
raw and whole.

And being clear and honest with it all,
together,
independently as one.

As Rumi once said, our work is only
to remove all the barriers between
us and love.

And those barriers are our fears.

As our bodies dip and roll,
Our minds begin to spin.
What if?
What if?
What if?

And we begin to erect

a million tiny defenses that protect
the divine truth of our being
from dancing in the light.

Afraid that if we don't hide
and shelter who we are
that we will be filleted,
exposed,
and cut to the bone.

Yet the truth is
the more we shelter,
the more we hide,
the more we seek safety,
and comfort,
and certainty,
the more we will deny ourselves
the grandest experience yet,
to be in and of love,
our most natural state of being.

And while I know in myself,
I have honed and refined
a fantastic set of defenses and beliefs,
and a million ways to construct
what I believe should happen,
and how, and when,
all that remains is
when I give myself permission with grace and faith
to be here now with you,
I delight in endless, divine joy.

Real.
Being.
Authentic.
Alive.
Love.

It is what it is, sweet darling.

AND I AM FREE

Oh to be free.

I used to believe that being free
meant I could do whatever I wanted.
Rebel against the tides
of "we've always done it that way,"
take foolhardy risks,
seize defyingly impossible opportunities.

And I did.

And I patted my own back
for my courage and accomplishments.

But it sank in that I was not free,
only determined.

I believed next that being free meant
I could say whatever I wanted.
Blast fiery statements,
use the c-word a lot...
A lot, a lot.

Empty every skeleton from my closet
and share all the gory details.

And I did.

And I patted my own back for my audacity
and truth telling.

But it sank in to me that I was not free,
only highly verbal and expressive.

One day, I stopped believing in being free.

I started breathing.

Here.
Now.
In this present moment.

The peace that washed me
through and through,
cleansing, clearing, and purifying,
settled in that to be free
is to be alive
and unencumbered by my beliefs.

It is my mind at ease,
silent.

And the seeking stopped.

And now, I believe only in the mystery of this life.

It is what it is.
And I am free.

TO BE ALIVE

When my dad died,
my perceived world came to a halt.

In his death, the superficial facade
of what I thought life was,
success, achievement, money,
status, and social hierarchy shattered.

Confronting the deep aching pain
of his loss changed me.

I began a long and arduous journey
of disassembling all the illusionary beliefs
and their origins in me
that set up such a false idolatry of a life lived.

When my physical life
in this little body met it's own ending,
my pending death pierced through the illusion
that this life of healing
and breaking apart my beliefs
was so dreadingly serious.

It's almost laughable now.
And each moment at home
with my kids and our busy farm life
makes me giggle endlessly.

All we do is play and tease,
and joke,
dance and sing,
and find silliness tucked
in every moment.

And they are loved

with every ounce of energy
I've got.

There is not much more than this, ever.

To be alive.
To share in our joys.
To feel it all.
To be in love.

Letting go of every little touch of time,
progress chirped by the mind.

To let your heart in all its wisdom lead.
For a life will unfold in magic and miracles,

Peace and Joy.

LOVE IN MOTION

When I was 18 I tattooed the word "strength"
on my right foot along the bridge of my toes.

Perhaps, a part of me knew
that it would be required
to walk the path ahead.

For a lot of my life,
I believed being strong
was not only necessary
but meant exerting power,
showing no weakness,
no vulnerabilities of any kind.

If I can control the outcome,
dominate the situation,
get my way, essentially,
I was powerful.

Bad bitch vibes.

I came in hot with big energy
and a high level of pressure
which meant that a lot of people
who would rather avoid conflict acquiesced
further edifying my false belief
that I was, indeed, powerful
and these people were weak.

Really, I was just controlling.

And I was deeply afraid of my own powerlessness.

Over the last 15 years working and coaching
I've learned that when you feel powerless,

not powerful,
you will exert everything you can
outside of yourself
to intimidate people and circumstances,
climb corporate ladders with avarice,
and demand absolute fealty
from those around you.

You will manipulate,
assert dominance,
and punish those who don't comply.

Amassing power is not a sign of inner strength
but fear and disconnection from oneself
and ones true guidance and purpose.

The truly powerful among us
know that real authority,
real guidance,
real leadership
comes from giving power away.

It is the inner strength to not exert your will,
but instead allow others to expand
into their fullest capacity
and tap their own strength,
creativity, and wisdom.

The most powerful people
are the ones who surrender
to be of service to the whole,
the betterment of what is mutually-beneficial,
the big vision of an organization,
and it is rooted in love.

They do not inspire fear
because they have no desire
to dominate or control.

Instead, you will know when you are
in the presence of a truly powerful person
because you become more yourself,
and more empowered to be yourself.

And now my work does not
come from bullying my way
into a better position,
but rather the strength
to humble myself each day
to be in service,
in devotion to the whole.

It is not easy,
and I fail frequently,
and must continue to check myself
each step of the way
when my ego wants
to deny the power of another,
their perspective,
their autonomy,
to choose what is best for them,
or best for us,
or best for the whole.

This is real courage.
This is real bravery.
This is real strength.

This is the only power that matters,
and it pours from one heart to the next.
The only power that cannot be conquered,
love in motion,
love in devotion.

THE ONLY EMOTION IS LOVE

I walked out of the front door
of my parents house,
hopped off the front deck,
walked down the hill around
the west side of their house,
back to the shelter belt by the rust red barn.

My dad was standing there
with my half brother talking.
They were working on something,
a project for hunting or fixing up
an estate sale find.

My dad saw me and his blue eyes lit up.

He had the clearest blue eyes.
Paul Newman eyes.

His smile bright as he walked towards me,
"Ashley! You're here!"

He put his arm around my shoulder and
we started back towards the house,
headed for the garage looking
for tool he needed.

As we walked, he looked at me and said,
"Ashley, the only emotion is love."

He hugged me and as quickly as he said it,
the moment faded
… and I woke up.

This is the dream I had days after my dad died.

It stays with me every moment of every day.

I believe in every part of my body
that it wasn't my unconscious processing,
but truly my dad,
his energy, his presence,
delivering this message
that I so desperately needed
to hear in my grief.

I could feel and know it was him.

At the time, I thought it was a message
to help my heart heal the massive hole
from where he once was.

Years later, I know that this
wasn't a message of consoling,
but an edict,
a mission,
my purpose delivered.

To live a life of love:
unconditional and universal love.

It is the experience of this love
that offers us
tremendous healing,
grace and peace.

A liberation from our deepest suffering.

And so I ask myself every day:
how can I do this in love?

how can I open my heart in love when I want to shut
down?

how can I offer an experience of love to everyone I
meet?

how do I live in love?

I fail at this most days.

But every day begins again
with the opportunity
to show up in love.

Love for me.
Love for you.

I am love,
so are you.

THE DEPTH OF SILENT LOVE

I used to think that I only swam in the depths.

I wanted to know every atom of who you are.
What makes you tick?

I wanted to talk and talk
until we ran out of things to say.
I used to think anything but
was living life in the dull shallows.

Superficial facades and small talk bored me to death.

Until I came to know that
I've never known a love so sweet
and complete
but to be with you in silence
with not a word shared,
only a look of your total presence.

This is all I wanted all along.

To be.
To be with you.

And not in the way where I needed
to spill my every secret
and still find your acceptance
to be fully seen, and heard, and valued.

No.

The most powerful truth and truest love
I've ever felt is one
in which I felt with my whole being
that your soul knew my soul,

with no words,
and no actions needed.

This was all there was and all there could be.

Pure connection.
Nothing more,
nothing less.

And it is everything.

INTEGRITY IN THE SPOTLIGHT

Integrity isn't solidified when no one is watching.

That's some weak sauce, bullshit.

Behind closed doors
when you are with yourself
and you make a difficult choice
but the one that honors what's "right"
its fucking easy.

Good on you, man, but a five-year-old knows
to push the shopping cart back
to the cart return even when no one is watching.

Nah, loves.

Integrity is shined with a spotlight
when you are on full display.

When you know that doing
the right thing is not the popular opinion.
When you know you are going
to displease others.

When you know that by standing
in truth you will stand alone...

And you don't tuck tail,
or win others' approval,
or split the difference in moderation.

Then and only then is your foundation solid.
Your structural integrity in check.

And truth always speaks.

The character of a man
isn't expressed in words.

Its actions.
Its consistency.
Its service to the dignity of others.
And this breeds character.

In the face of truth,
many will crumble.

The facade splits.
The dog and pony show is over.

And if you stand in support
of others with little integrity,
self-serving interests,
birds of a feather,
who you are is on bold display.

I'll say this for myself as well.

I've questioned my own character
and integrity in the last few years.

I saw what I saw
and I tried to find a truce.
Work around.
Soften edges.
Tiptoe across the eggshells.

I walked a tight rope
and I put myself
and my integrity in question.

Lesson learned.

My tolerance for bullshit
has become nothing this year.

And just as I stand for truth
with my own humility in hand
to be better every step of the way,
you show me your character
just the same.

And it's coming in hot.

THE LIBERATION OF SINCERITY

Sincerity.

It's a word that rolls with me all the time.

I can feel it pulse
and crawl under my skin,
sit on my tongue,
and hum in my mind.

It's a liberation
that frees one from the past
and the portions of our self
that may push us to judge,
defend, or become hypocritical.

The sincerity of our thought,
our words,
and our intentions
is freedom.

It's honest.
And authentic.
And soaked with our whole heart.

But it demands us to move
with our whole being.

To feel into each moment
and each other
in divine whole connection.

And in this openness,
we find joy
and sweet contentment.

All my love.

Sincerely,
Me.

PART IV: WILD AND UNBOUND

"The wound became a gift when I understood its message." Clarissa Pinkola Estés

THE GIFT OF BEING SEEN

I used to want to be seen,
heard, and valued.

I used to feel like no one
understood who I was.

And then I learned it was me.

I did not know myself,
and so no one else could know me either.

What I was seeking outside of myself
I could only give to my self.

And as I trenched
to the depths of my being,
understanding how I saw the world,
why I saw the world in this way,
and what happened throughout my lifetime
to create the conditioning of my lens on life,
I ripped apart all my foundations.

I shed one limiting belief after another.

I shed self destruction,
self hatred,
self denial,
self violence,
self pity,
Self.

As each remnant of my self crumbled away,
I began to move each day.

I've died and been reborn a thousand times.

And I'll never stop.

There is no self to know.
There is only the brilliance
of this beautiful existence
we are blessed to share with one another.

It's a moment in time.

And I don't seek to see you either.

I won't judge, or limit, or deny,
or demand you be something
you are not
or could be.

And now we can breathe.

What a joy and a delight to be
You.
and
Me.

LEAP INTO FULLNESS

Will you believe before there is evidence?
Will you trust before there is proof?
Will you leap the void before you look below?
Will you love before you feel it return to you?

This is what it means to be
fully embodied in this moment.

This is what it means to live
without holding anything back.

This is what it means to share
the truth of your heart in fullness,
the glory of you, my love.

Unguarded.
Unreactive.
Unafraid.

Believe.
Trust.
Leap.
Love.

SOUL SONG

Most people have no fucking clue what they are doing.

And when I realized this,
I set myself free.

After thousands of hours
of conversations with coaching clients
and really any person,
I am given the opportunity to
understand on a deeper level
you find out that most people
are generally dissatisfied
with some or all
of the life they are living.

Job is great, marriage is shit.
Job is shit, family is great.

Don't really love the place they live.
Feel stifled by responsibility.

And for a surprisingly large amount
the dissatisfaction is unidentifiable.

Just a low, dull, gnawing feeling that this life feels flat.

They aren't experiencing all it has to offer.
They aren't living their dreams
and their truest soul-stirring passions.
They are alive but asleep at the wheel.
Cruising towards aimless goals
without a real sense of purpose.

And most are deathly afraid
of what other people would say

if they dared to break out
of the box they are in
and live the life that truly sets
their hearts on fire.

And this teeny speck of knowledge
has become the key that unlocked freedom.

Because I also believe in my bones
it's unwise to follow others
who don't have experience
doing what I want to do.

If friends, family, coworkers are living
these lives of quiet desperation
as Thoreau once said,
then these are absolutely not
the opinions we use to guide
our life decisions by.

Thanks, but no thanks.
We don't give a fuck.

If you are inspired to break the mold,
live your own soul song,
pursue a destiny
you are uniquely passionate about
do exactly this.

And pay no mind to people
even the successful ones
who are defining a life well-lived
by a standard that is not your own.

Set yourself free, baby.

The world needs your gifts.
Your talents.
Your ideas and inspiration.

We need you in all your god-given glory.

Do the damn thing already.

EVERYTHING AND NOTHING

This life is everything
and nothing
all in the same moment
and it all ends
and begins again
in a different form
in the exact same way

The essence is:
Can you be totally detached from the life
you are living while completely immersed
in it every waking second?

This is the secret.
This is the magic
and the mystery.

Can you see that it is all just one giant game
and gleefully play your role to the hilt?

Can you risk it all, challenge yourself,
grind and soar to heights of your own success
and creativity unimaginable
all while knowing it is utterly meaningless?

This is it.

And in this way you access bliss
and joy that never stops
even through the heartache and sadness,
suffering and sometimes grief,
there is still joy and heart-bursting love
because we,
you and I,
are alive fully,

wild and unconfined,
while sometimes living an utterly ordinary life.

What an absolute miracle.

You are an absolute miracle.

This life is an absolute miracle.

Forever in awe.
Forever inspired.
Forever in love.

LIVE

We are so afraid of feeling
what we are feeling
because are terrified of our own bodies
and we are terrified of being alive.

We are terrified of our basic nature.
We are terrified that our feelings
may overwhelm us.
We are terrified of our humanity.

So we lie to ourselves and each other.
We tell ourselves that feeling is weakness.
And we happily retreat into our minds.

Creating false constructs of rigid ideologies
that pretend to give us a way
of navigating the world,
instead of following the built-in compass
that is our living, feeling, breathing body.

And when we live from our minds,
we make rules,
hold ideas and belief systems,
and these constructs force us into
living very shallow lives,
like flat rocks skimming the surface
unable to reach any real depth.

We create checklists for what makes
good and bad people.
We scan for superficial markers
of success as means of evaluation.

We judge peoples' jobs,
their attractiveness,

and their social circles.

And then we are shocked and horrified
that the superficial life we are living
is soul-sucking,
devoid of meaning and purpose,
shallow and vapid.

And that people are assessing us
for the same shallow reasons
and discarding us
when something better comes along.

It is the forever push-pull of gnawing dissatisfaction.

Because we are not seen and loved through
for all of who we are.

And yet, equally afraid
to allow the intimacy
of being held and loved
in a deeply meaningful and rich way
inviting an experience of feeling
that we have tried to escape
from most of our lives.

And we suffer.

We suffer greatly.

We avoid anything
and anyone that will puncture
our false, hollow narrative that pushes us
from our minds into our bodies.

Truth: there is only one freedom
and that is to move deeply into our bodies.

To feel every moment.

Surrender to a life
so big, rich, and full
it will shatter any illusion
of our minds and lukewarm living.

The only way out is through.

Feel it all,
be it all,
wild and free,
utterly consumed
by this experience
of being alive
in a breathing, feeling, primal
body.

LIVE WIRE

There is a piece of art has hung on my walls for years:
"If she's amazing she won't be easy."

I thought because I was broken in
so many ways that I had
collected traumas that made me
a wrecking ball to other people.

A walking paradoxical contrast
that learned to temper my fiery fierceness
with measured, thoughtful responses
with sugary, syrupy sweetness
and professional candor.

I healed through the once
mean-spirited, reactionary lashing-out
and gave birth to quiet invitations
to my displeasure and dissatisfaction.

Often though, I just sat in silence watching.
Observing, noting, patiently waiting.

Softening every sharp edge on my being
as I spent the lonely roads
into the pits of my trauma
unearthing dense, old, aching pain
and silently holding new, fresh hurts.

"See look at me!
It's not that I'm hard to be with
because I carried so much
of my past with me,
see I'm so sweet and soft now!"

Now, I am easy to be with.

But in truth, I'm not.

What I didn't realize
is that I was actually easier
to be with back then.

I was highly predictable.
Say nothing for months on end
and then explode
and we can sweep it under the rug
because I felt ashamed for unhinging
and being the shit person
while the neglect and hurts perpetuate.

For me to let this continue,
I had to slide back into sour numbness.

Now, I am not easy
because I've lost every trace
of every last filter
and being here with me
means walking through it all with me.

I can't hide it on my face.
I can't hide it in my voice.

My whole body vibrates with every moment.

My passion, my pleasure,
my seductive joy
and every ache of my sadness,
and hurt, and pain.

I'm not easy now
because to walk with me
is to plunge to the depths of this moment,
not just the shiny speckles
that I've honed and refined
after I've healed in silence.

Nah, Loves.

We do this together now in real time.

And the electricity that pulses through
every bit of my being
as lightning in a bottle
makes being alive ecstasy incarnate.

But you gotta be able to hold a live wire.

Because she's not easy.

A BEAUTIFUL PARADOX

When Shae was a baby
she was impossible to get to sleep.
But once she was down,
she would sleep all night.

I learned the magic was
with the softest touch
I could find breath through the tips
of my fingers to her forehead,
skimming the bridge of her nose.

I was gently gliding my fingers
across her face for hours.
When I think of who I am
this is me.

And yet, I have a rolling, ferocious fire
that burns in my belly.
Quakes me from my sleep.

The ferocity, while it is me too,
hardens my heart.

Being all of 5'1,
I've often embodied
the stereotype of being a spitfire.

Fully loaded.
Palpably intense.
Firecracker.

The only reason
I have this capacity is
because I've had to fight,
and claw,

and hold my own every step of the way.

But the truest pieces of me
are as gentle as sweet can be.

Because when I embody all that I am
it's lullabies and silly songs
and explosions of passion,
creation, and drive.

And in this world of labels
and definitions of our selfhood,
we often try to frame
the woman before us.

Is she the good girl?
Or the difficult bitch?

Perhaps, we would all do better
tucking away our self-imposed
and projected definitions
and hold them all.

A delicious paradox.

That day by day by day,
we embody it all.
We are it all.

And it's a massive fucking
contradiction consecrated
on our voyage
through this life.

But what an unfathomable delight.
In this way, I see you

One messy contradiction
layered on top of the next.

All of you.

Perfectly divine.

TO THE EDGE

Love will destroy you.
Love will shatter you.
Love will take you the edge
and break you again,
and again.

And this is precisely the point.

And how exquisitely beautiful it is.
Not in a sadist sort of way or
a hopeless romantic sort of way.

But in the most honest way.

Your being,
soul,
heart falls in love
and loves your people.

Sees the beauty in every being
and divinity reflected back to you.
Wants the deepest, luscious rich
unending waves of love
colliding and washing
through your whole being.

To be and vibrate love.

And you,
your identity,
your self,
your ego
is the facade that stands
between your soul
and this deepest desire.

And now love will destroy
all of your false, illusions of you.

Love will shatter any limitations
you've created to protect your heart.

Love will take you to the edge
of your pain and heartache,
and break each shell
until your softness is exposed again.

This is the awesome power
of your love,
and loving another.

Mother and child.
Dearest friend.
Life-long lover.

The more your resist,
the more brutal love is.

And most people don't realize
that the ever-unfolding drama
of their lives is exactly this:

Love finding any and every way to flow.
Love brings us back home to our truth always.

Boldly destroying everything that does not serve.

How unbelievably brilliant
and dangerously beautiful.

THE WILD JOY OF BEING

There comes a point when we realize
that the glory of this life is to be alive.

In sheer gratitude for this moment.
That's all.
To be alive.

We are no longer willing to protect ourselves
to avoid feeling the difficult feelings.

We are no longer willing
to spill our guts across the floor
to appease others
or project ourselves upon them.

We just are.
We live.
We breathe.
We love.

We know that through a litany of circumstances
and experiences as we mix with a million
contradictions
and possibilities that life will unfold exactly
as it does.

Without judgement.
Without victimization.
Without denial.
Without intellectualization.

What a maddening joy
to be alive with you here.

Forever wildly amused.

Forever blissed the fuck out
in my thankfulness for today.

WILD AND UNBOUND

My mom says the one thing
she has always known
to be true about me
is that I cannot stand to be caged in.

Like a panther uneasily pacing
the glass barrier at the zoo,
my soul revolts against confinement.

And I've run many, many, many times.

People closest to me
know that when I am done,
I'm done,
and you are dead to me.

I rarely re-open any door
when I believe someone desires
to control me.

I vividly remember after an epic fight,
driving for hours,
up and down,
back and forth
country roads by my farm
wanting to flee off into the night,
telling myself,
"you can make it to Chicago in 8 hours."

Often dreaming of sliding
into a new town
with a new name
and disappearing from all that has trapped me in.

That day, I drove to Target

and bought a tent,
popped it up in the backyard for six weeks,
and slept there every night.

I was divorced a few months later.

The one thing that stills burns in me
with my unending desire for freedom,
to move, and grow, and go,
and run and run and run
is my people.

Oh god, do I love with every bit of my being.

So I always return.

I settle in and find peace
in the choice that I make
to be here now.

And the truth is that I love people,
not just my own,
but all people
with such a shaking awe
and reverence that quiets
my urge to fly with wings to the sky.

And this is what I know,
I fucking hate being controlled
and tied down,
and trapped,
and cornered,
but oh boy,
I will stay here for you
until the end of time.

All my love to you,
always and forever.

ACKNOWLEDGEMENTS

To my dad— You were my first home in this world. Your love grounded me. Your presence softened what could have broken me. Losing you shattered me open, but it also woke me up. You are in these pages. You are in everything I've become.

To my children— You are my reason. My teachers. My joy. You are why I healed. You remind me every day that love is real, and that it's worth living for.

www.ingramcontent.com/pod-product-compliance
Lightning Source LLC
Chambersburg PA
CBHW070341130626
46556CB00007B/2968